AFTER YOU

A Journey through the
First Year of Bereavement

MARYALICIA POST

Contents

February

This is the last night I will watch you sleep
This is the last night
This is
Death closer than I
Drops of water more compassionate
Than kisses
I am your twin caught in the womb
You were called first
Helpless, you leave me
Through my final whisper
Your first silence
Only my heart beats
Heartless

March

Like a kite's tail whipped in the wind
One word snaps behind each thought
Never
Cold morning alone in our bed
No memories coming
Let me in
Once you called me by my name in the ordinary way
For the last time
When?
You were the benchmark for my distances
How will I find home
Again

April

First warm day since your going
Spring flowers mindlessly blossom
Such confusion
First rain since you left
You would have said 'the farmers need it'
Such silence
Outlived by daffodils, shoes, jobs begun
Mortality rules
Okay

May

Anxious for morning
I run towards it in the dark
And fall heavily
When dawn comes in its own time
I'll have bruises to show
For my haste

June

Sometimes now the fog lifts
And I see the shore
But my boat has no oars
And days are sails which fail to catch the
Wind
I'll sleep
The tide must turn soon

July

Am I me or you? I can't remember
This food
Your favourite or mine?
Here's an equation;
When two become one
Take away one leaves zero

August

Six months now
Still yearning, still learning
Still running, still falling
Still here
Each night inventing the courage
To cross the dark doorsill
Into sleep

September

How portable grief is
I carry mine like a music box
And play
Its thin sharp melody
In all the silent places
Of the day

October

You belong to the sea now
Ashes dissolved
Like salt in the water
But when I search for you
It's the sky my eyes implore
To give you back

November

Since my heart became an orphan
Kindly people
Offer it shelter
They move chairs closer
At the table of their days
To make room for it
A grateful guest
It longs to feel better
If only for its host's sake

December

Walking from the shops
In windy dark
Frozen dinner bagged in plastic
Suddenly, for no reason
Joy stirs in its sleep
I sense
Brightness
Like the first bead of water
Swelling from a rusty tap

January

The snowdrops you planted
For me
Are blooming again in the garden

AFTER WORDS

This second edition of *After You* offers me the chance to say something about 'how long this lasts' — how long before I felt whole again, how long before the cloud of grief lifted. I began to notice signs of a real change in five years. That's when I began to feel like an entire, viable person again.

The first sign was being able to came home to a dark and empty house without a qualm. I noticed kind Dublin taxi drivers stopped waiting to see me unlock my door and watch me go inside so I must have seemed more confident even to an observer. I still wore my wedding ring and in fact I still do, but describing myself as Ms instead of Mrs has become automatic and causes me no pain.

I talk about my husband often to his grandchildren, one of whom was born after he died, telling them stories about his life and our life together. He is as real to them as he is to me though to be honest perhaps a bit of a legendary figure. My grandson — he was about seven at the time—once asked me to tell him about WW2... 'What do you already know about it?' I asked him.. 'It was a big war and grandad won it', he answered.

I know the time it takes to heal varies with the individual, but all these years later I see this is how it was for me. In time, pain disappeared but love remained. It was a long journey, but I reached a peaceful shore.

I wish the same for you.

Maryalicia

Other books by this author

This Life: a love story

Sky Full of Clouds

Death of an Adult Child

ARC

Website:

maryaliciapost.com